HAL•LEONARD

JAZZ PLAY-ALONG®

Book & Audio for B♭, E♭, C and Bass Clef Instruments

volume 111

Arranged and Produced by Mark Taylor

Cool Christmas
10 Timeless Favorites

PLAYBACK+
Speed • Pitch • Balance • Loop

To access audio, visit:
www.halleonard.com/mylibrary

Enter Code
2038-3471-0827-1077

ISBN 978-1-4234-8253-6

HAL•LEONARD®

Visit Hal Leonard Online at
www.halleonard.com

World headquarters, contact:
Hal Leonard
7777 West Bluemound Road
Milwaukee, WI 53213
Email: info@halleonard.com

In Europe, contact:
Hal Leonard Europe Limited
1 Red Place
London, W1K 6PL
Email: info@halleonardeurope.com

In Australia, contact:
Hal Leonard Australia Pty. Ltd.
4 Lentara Court
Cheltenham, Victoria, 3192 Australia
Email: info@halleonard.com.au

COOL CHRISTMAS

Volume 111

Arranged and Produced by
Mark Taylor

Featured Players:

Graham Breedlove–Trumpet
John Desalme–Tenor Saxophone
Tony Nalker–Piano
Jim Roberts–Bass
Todd Harrison–Drums

Recorded at Bias Studios, Springfield, Virginia
Bob Dawson, Engineer

HOW TO USE THE AUDIO:

Each song has <u>two</u> tracks:

1) Split Track/Demonstration

Woodwind, Brass, Keyboard, and **Mallet Players** can use this track as a learning tool for melody style and inflection.

Bass Players can learn and perform with this track – remove the recorded bass track by turning down the volume on the LEFT channel.

Keyboard and **Guitar Players** can learn and perform with this track – remove the recorded piano part by turning down the volume on the RIGHT channel.

2) Backing Track

Soloists or **Groups** can learn and perform with this accompaniment track with the RHYTHM SECTION only.

AULD LANG SYNE

WORDS BY ROBERT BURNS
TRADITIONAL SCOTTISH MELODY

C VERSION

DECK THE HALL

TRADITIONAL WELSH CAROL

C VERSION

O CHRISTMAS TREE

Traditional German Carol

C Version

THE FIRST NOËL

17TH CENTURY ENGLISH CAROL
MUSIC FROM W. SANDYS' CHRISTMAS CAROLS

C VERSION

9

GOOD KING WENCESLAS

WORDS BY JOHN M. NEALE
MUSIC FROM PIAE CANTIONES

C VERSION

Jingle Bells

WORDS AND MUSIC BY
J. PIERPONT

C VERSION

TOYLAND

WORDS BY GLEN MACDONOUGH
MUSIC BY VICTOR HERBERT

C VERSION

UP ON THE HOUSETOP

WORDS AND MUSIC BY
B.R. HANBY

C VERSION

WE THREE KINGS OF ORIENT ARE

WORDS AND MUSIC BY
JOHN H. HOPKINS, JR.

C VERSION

WE WISH YOU A MERRY CHRISTMAS

C VERSION

TRADITIONAL ENGLISH FOLKSONG

AULD LANG SYNE

WORDS BY ROBERT BURNS
TRADITIONAL SCOTTISH MELODY

DECK THE HALL

TRADITIONAL WELSH CAROL

Bb VERSION

O Christmas Tree

Traditional German Carol

THE FIRST NOËL

17TH CENTURY ENGLISH CAROL
MUSIC FROM W. SANDYS' CHRISTMAS CAROLS

Bb VERSION

GOOD KING WENCESLAS

WORDS BY JOHN M. NEALE
MUSIC FROM PIAE CANTIONES

Bb VERSION

27

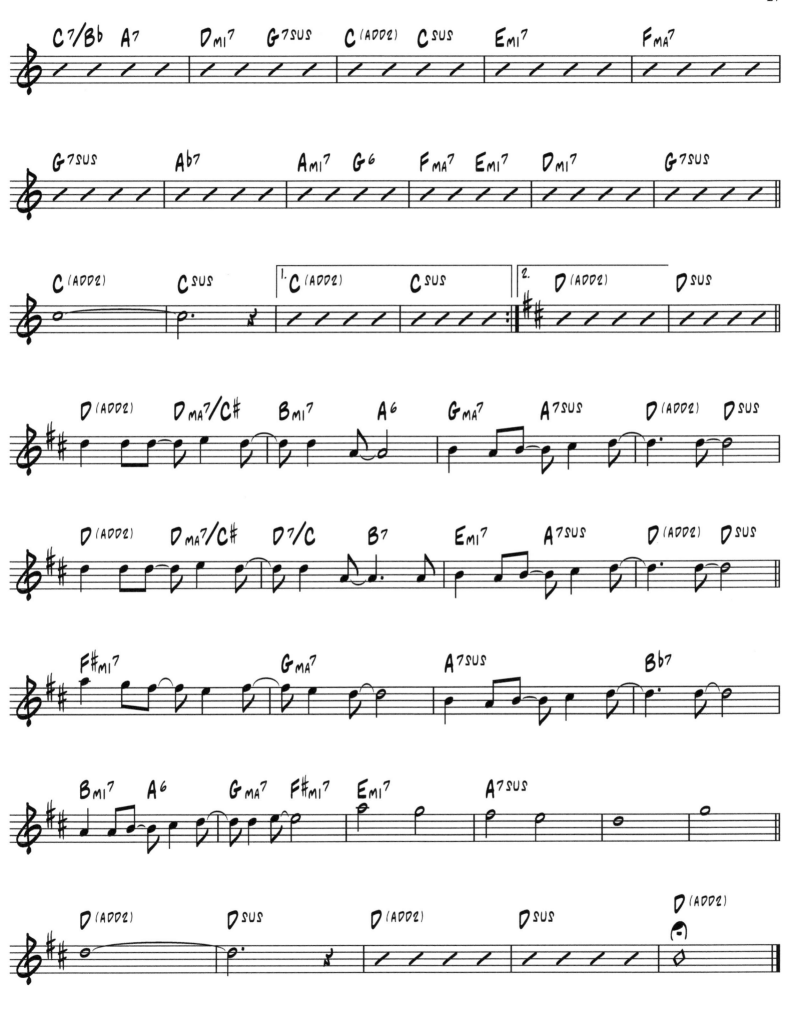

Jingle Bells

WORDS AND MUSIC BY
J. PIERPONT

Bb VERSION

TOYLAND

WORDS BY GLEN MACDONOUGH
MUSIC BY VICTOR HERBERT

Bb VERSION

UP ON THE HOUSETOP

WORDS AND MUSIC BY
B.R. HANBY

WE THREE KINGS OF ORIENT ARE

WORDS AND MUSIC BY
JOHN H. HOPKINS, JR.

Bb VERSION

WE WISH YOU A MERRY CHRISTMAS

Bb Version

Traditional English Folksong

AULD LANG SYNE

WORDS BY ROBERT BURNS
TRADITIONAL SCOTTISH MELODY

Eb VERSION

DECK THE HALL

TRADITIONAL WELSH CAROL

Eb VERSION

O Christmas Tree

TRADITIONAL GERMAN CAROL

The First Noël

17TH CENTURY ENGLISH CAROL
MUSIC FROM W. SANDYS' CHRISTMAS CAROLS

Eb VERSION

Good King Wenceslas

WORDS BY JOHN M. NEALE
MUSIC FROM PIAE CANTIONES

Eb VERSION

43

Jingle Bells

WORDS AND MUSIC BY
J. PIERPONT

TOYLAND

WORDS BY GLEN MACDONOUGH
MUSIC BY VICTOR HERBERT

Eb VERSION

UP ON THE HOUSETOP

WORDS AND MUSIC BY
B.R. HANBY

WE THREE KINGS OF ORIENT ARE

WORDS AND MUSIC BY
JOHN H. HOPKINS, JR.

Eb VERSION

WE WISH YOU A MERRY CHRISTMAS

Eb Version

TRADITIONAL ENGLISH FOLKSONG

AULD LANG SYNE

WORDS BY ROBERT BURNS
TRADITIONAL SCOTTISH MELODY

DECK THE HALL

TRADITIONAL WELSH CAROL

O Christmas Tree

Traditional German Carol

THE FIRST NOËL

17TH CENTURY ENGLISH CAROL
MUSIC FROM W. SANDYS' CHRISTMAS CAROLS

GOOD KING WENCESLAS

WORDS BY JOHN M. NEALE
MUSIC FROM PIAE CANTIONES

Jingle Bells

WORDS AND MUSIC BY
J. PIERPONT

TOYLAND

WORDS BY GLEN MACDONOUGH
MUSIC BY VICTOR HERBERT

C VERSION

UP ON THE HOUSETOP

WORDS AND MUSIC BY
B.R. HANBY

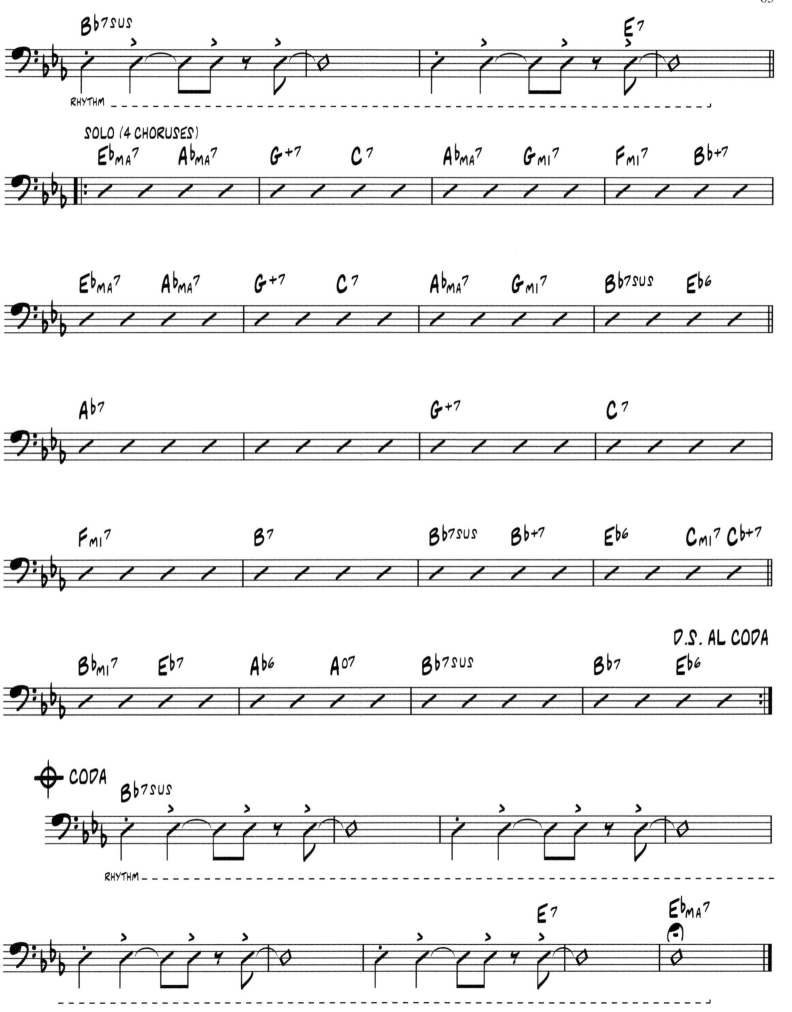

We Three Kings of Orient Are

WORDS AND MUSIC BY
JOHN H. HOPKINS, JR.

WE WISH YOU A MERRY CHRISTMAS

C VERSION

TRADITIONAL ENGLISH FOLKSONG

The Best-Selling Jazz Book of All Time Is Now Legal!

The Real Books are the most popular jazz books of all time. Since the 1970s, musicians have trusted these volumes to get them through every gig, night after night. The problem is that the books were illegally produced and distributed, without any regard to copyright law, or royalties paid to the composers who created these musical masterpieces.

Hal Leonard is very proud to present the first legitimate and legal editions of these books ever produced. You won't even notice the difference, other than all the notorious errors being fixed: the covers and typeface look the same, the song lists are nearly identical, and the price for our edition is even cheaper than the originals!

Every conscientious musician will appreciate that these books are now produced accurately and ethically, benefitting the songwriters that we owe for some of the greatest tunes of all time!

VOLUME 1
00240221	C Edition	$49.99
00240224	B♭ Edition	$49.99
00240225	E♭ Edition	$49.99
00240226	Bass Clef Edition	$49.99
00286389	F Edition	$39.99
00240292	C Edition 6 x 9	$39.99
00240339	B♭ Edition 6 x 9	$44.99
00147792	Bass Clef Edition 6 x 9	$39.99
00200984	Online Backing Tracks: Selections	$45.00
00110604	Book/USB Flash Drive Backing Tracks Pack	$85.00
00110599	USB Flash Drive Only	$50.00

VOLUME 2
00240222	C Edition	$49.99
00240227	B♭ Edition	$49.99
00240228	E♭ Edition	$49.99
00240229	Bass Clef Edition	$49.99
00240293	C Edition 6 x 9	$39.99
00125900	B♭ Edition 6 x 9	$39.99
00125900	The Real Book – Mini Edition	$39.99
00204126	Backing Tracks on USB Flash Drive	$55.00
00204131	C Edition – USB Flash Drive Pack	$85.00

VOLUME 3
00240233	C Edition	$49.99
00240284	B♭ Edition	$49.99
00240285	E♭ Edition	$49.99
00240286	Bass Clef Edition	$49.99
00240338	C Edition 6 x 9	$39.99

VOLUME 4
00240296	C Edition	$49.99
00103348	B♭ Edition	$49.99
00103349	E♭ Edition	$49.99
00103350	Bass Clef Edition	$49.99

VOLUME 5
00240349	C Edition	$49.99
00175278	B♭ Edition	$49.99
00175279	E♭ Edition	$49.99

VOLUME 6
00240534	C Edition	$49.99
00223637	E♭ Edition	$49.99

Also available:
00154230	The Real Bebop Book C Edition	$34.99
00295069	The Real Bebop Book E♭ Edition	$34.99
00295068	The Real Bebop Book B♭ Edition	$34.99
00240264	The Real Blues Book	$39.99
00310910	The Real Bluegrass Book	$39.99
00240223	The Real Broadway Book	$39.99
00240440	The Trane Book	$25.00
00125426	The Real Country Book	$45.00
00269721	The Real Miles Davis Book C Edition	$29.99
00269723	The Real Miles Davis Book B♭ Edition	$29.99
00240355	The Real Dixieland Book C Edition	$39.99
00294853	The Real Dixieland Book E♭ Edition	$39.99
00122335	The Real Dixieland Book B♭ Edition	$39.99
00240235	The Duke Ellington Real Book	$29.99
00240268	The Real Jazz Solos Book	$44.99
00240348	The Real Latin Book C Edition	$39.99
00127107	The Real Latin Book B♭ Edition	$39.99
00120809	The Pat Metheny Real Book C Edition	$34.99
00252119	The Pat Metheny Real Book B♭ Edition	$29.99
00240358	The Charlie Parker Real Book C Edition	$25.00
00275997	The Charlie Parker Real Book E♭ Edition	$25.00
00118324	The Real Pop Book C Edition – Vol. 1	$45.00
00295066	The Real Pop Book B♭ Edition – Vol. 1	$39.99
00286451	The Real Pop Book C Edition – Vol. 2	$45.00
00240331	The Bud Powell Real Book	$25.00
00240437	The Real R&B Book C Edition	$45.00
00276590	The Real R&B Book B♭ Edition	$45.00
00240313	The Real Rock Book	$39.99
00240323	The Real Rock Book – Vol. 2	$39.99
00240359	The Real Tab Book	$39.99
00240317	The Real Worship Book	$35.00

THE REAL CHRISTMAS BOOK
00240306	C Edition	$39.99
00240345	B♭ Edition	$35.00
00240346	E♭ Edition	$35.00
00240347	Bass Clef Edition	$35.00

THE REAL VOCAL BOOK
00240230	Volume 1 High Voice	$40.00
00240307	Volume 1 Low Voice	$40.00
00240231	Volume 2 High Voice	$39.99
00240308	Volume 2 Low Voice	$39.99
00240391	Volume 3 High Voice	$39.99
00240392	Volume 3 Low Voice	$39.99
00118318	Volume 4 High Voice	$39.99
00118319	Volume 4 Low Voice	$39.99

Complete song lists online at www.halleonard.com

Prices, content, and availability subject to change without notice.

HAL•LEONARD®

0223
318

CHRISTMAS COLLECTIONS
FROM HAL LEONARD
ALL BOOKS ARRANGED FOR PIANO, VOICE & GUITAR

THE BEST CHRISTMAS SONGS EVER
69 all-time favorites: Auld Lang Syne • Coventry Carol • Frosty the Snow Man • Happy Holiday • It Came Upon the Midnight Clear • O Holy Night • Rudolph the Red-Nosed Reindeer • Silver Bells • What Child Is This? • and many more.
00359130 ....$29.99

THE BIG BOOK OF CHRISTMAS SONGS
Over 120 all-time favorites and hard-to-find classics: As Each Happy Christmas • The Boar's Head Carol • Carol of the Bells • Deck the Halls • The Friendly Beasts • God Rest Ye Merry Gentlemen • Joy to the World • Masters in This Hall • O Holy Night • Story of the Shepherd • and more.
00311520 ....$22.99

CHRISTMAS SONGS – BUDGET BOOKS
100 holiday favorites: All I Want for Christmas Is You • Christmas Time Is Here • Feliz Navidad • Grandma Got Run Over by a Reindeer • I'll Be Home for Christmas • Last Christmas • O Holy Night • Please Come Home for Christmas • Rockin' Around the Christmas Tree • We Need a Little Christmas • What Child Is This? • and more.
00310887 ....$15.99

CHRISTMAS MOVIE SONGS
34 holiday hits from the big screen: All I Want for Christmas Is You • Believe • Christmas Vacation • Do You Want to Build a Snowman? • Frosty the Snow Man • Have Yourself a Merry Little Christmas • It's Beginning to Look like Christmas • Mele Kalikimaka • Rudolph the Red-Nosed Reindeer • Silver Bells • White Christmas • You're a Mean One, Mr. Grinch • and more.
00146961 ....$19.99

CHRISTMAS POP STANDARDS
22 contemporary holiday hits, including: All I Want for Christmas Is You • Christmas Time Is Here • Little Saint Nick • Mary, Did You Know? • Merry Christmas, Darling • Santa Baby • Underneath the Tree • Where Are You Christmas? • and more.
00348998 ....$14.99

CHRISTMAS SING-ALONG
40 seasonal favorites: Away in a Manger • Christmas Time Is Here • Feliz Navidad • Happy Holiday • Jingle Bells • Mary, Did You Know? • O Come, All Ye Faithful • Rudolph the Red-Nosed Reindeer • Silent Night • White Christmas • and more. Includes online sing-along backing tracks.
00278176 Book/Online Audio $24.99

100 CHRISTMAS CAROLS
Includes: Away in a Manger • Bring a Torch, Jeannette, Isabella • Coventry Carol • Deck the Hall • The First Noel • Go, Tell It on the Mountain • I Heard the Bells on Christmas Day • Joy to the World • O Come, All Ye Faithful (Adeste Fideles) • Silent Night • and more.
00310897 ....$19.99

100 MOST BEAUTIFUL CHRISTMAS SONGS
Includes: Angels We Have Heard on High • Baby, It's Cold Outside • Christmas Time Is Here • Do You Hear What I Hear • Grown-Up Christmas List • Happy Xmas (War Is Over) • I'll Be Home for Christmas • The Little Drummer Boy • Mary, Did You Know? • O Holy Night • White Christmas • Winter Wonderland • and more.
00237285 ....$29.99

MOST-STREAMED CHRISTMAS SONGS
Includes: All I Want for Christmas Is You • Blue Christmas • Christmas (Baby Please Come Home) • Feliz Navidad • I'll Be Home for Christmas • It's Beginning to Look like Christmas • Jingle Bell Rock • Last Christmas • Mary, Did You Know? • Santa Baby • Santa Tell Me • Sleigh Ride • Underneath the Tree • White Christmas • and more.
00666189 ....$22.99

POPULAR CHRISTMAS SHEET MUSIC: 1980-2017
40 recent seasonal favorites: All I Want for Christmas Is You • Because It's Christmas (For All the Children) • Breath of Heaven (Mary's Song) • Christmas Lights • The Christmas Shoes • The Gift • Grown-Up Christmas List • Last Christmas • Santa Tell Me • Snowman • Where Are You Christmas? • Wrapped in Red • and more.
00278089 ....$22.99

A SENTIMENTAL CHRISTMAS BOOK
27 beloved Christmas favorites, including: The Christmas Shoes • The Christmas Song (Chestnuts Roasting on an Open Fire) • Christmas Time Is Here • Grown-Up Christmas List • Have Yourself a Merry Little Christmas • I'll Be Home for Christmas • Somewhere in My Memory • Where Are You Christmas? • and more.
00236830 ....$14.99

ULTIMATE CHRISTMAS
100 seasonal favorites: Auld Lang Syne • Bring a Torch, Jeannette, Isabella • Carol of the Bells • The Chipmunk Song • Christmas Time Is Here • The First Noel • Frosty the Snow Man • Gesù Bambino • Happy Holiday • Happy Xmas (War Is Over) • Jingle-Bell Rock • Pretty Paper • Silver Bells • Suzy Snowflake • and more.
00361399 ....$24.99

A VERY MERRY CHRISTMAS
39 familiar favorites: Blue Christmas • Feliz Navidad • Happy Xmas (War Is Over) • I'll Be Home for Christmas • Jingle-Bell Rock • Please Come Home for Christmas • Rockin' Around the Christmas Tree • Santa, Bring My Baby Back (To Me) • Sleigh Ride • White Christmas • and more.
00310536 ....$14.99

HAL•LEONARD®

Complete contents listings available online at www.halleonard.com

Prices, contents, and availability subject to change without notice.

JAZZ INSTRUCTION & IMPROVISATION

BOOKS FOR ALL INSTRUMENTS FROM HAL LEONARD

500 JAZZ LICKS
by Brent Vaartstra

This book aims to assist you on your journey to play jazz fluently. These short phrases and ideas we call "licks" will help you understand how to navigate the common chords and chord progressions you will encounter. Adding this vocabulary to your arsenal will send you down the right path and improve your jazz playing, regardless of your instrument.

00142384 ....$16.99

1001 JAZZ LICKS
by Jack Shneidman
Cherry Lane Music

This book presents 1,001 melodic gems played over dozens of the most important chord progressions heard in jazz. This is the ideal book for beginners seeking a well-organized, easy-to-follow encyclopedia of jazz vocabulary, as well as professionals who want to take their knowledge of the jazz language to new heights.

02500133 ....$17.99

THE BERKLEE BOOK OF JAZZ HARMONY
by Joe Mulholland & Tom Hojnacki

Learn jazz harmony, as taught at Berklee College of Music. This text provides a strong foundation in harmonic principles, supporting further study in jazz composition, arranging, and improvisation. It covers basic chord types and their tensions, with practical demonstrations of how they are used in characteristic jazz contexts and an accompanying recording that lets you hear how they can be applied.

00113755 Book/Online Audio........$34.99

BUILDING A JAZZ VOCABULARY
By Mike Steinel

A valuable resource for learning the basics of jazz from Mike Steinel of the University of North Texas. It covers: the basics of jazz • how to build effective solos • a comprehensive practice routine • and a jazz vocabulary of the masters.

00849911 ....$22.99

COMPREHENSIVE TECHNIQUE FOR JAZZ MUSICIANS
2ND EDITION
by Bert Ligon
Houston Publishing

An incredible presentation of the most practical exercises an aspiring jazz student could want. All are logically interwoven with the "real world" examples from jazz to classical. This book is an essential anthology of technical, compositional, and theoretical exercises, with lots of musical examples.

00030455 ....$34.99

EAR TRAINING
by Keith Wyatt, Carl Schroeder and Joe Elliott
Musicians Institute Press

Covers: basic pitch matching • singing major and minor scales • identifying intervals • transcribing melodies and rhythm • identifying chords and progressions • seventh chords and the blues • modal interchange, chromaticism, modulation • and more.

00695198 Book/Online Audio........$29.99

EXERCISES AND ETUDES FOR THE JAZZ INSTRUMENTALIST
by J.J. Johnson

Designed as study material and playable by any instrument, these pieces run the gamut of the jazz experience, featuring common and uncommon time signatures and keys, and styles from ballads to funk. They are progressively graded so that both beginners and professionals will be challenged by the demands of this wonderful music.

00842018 Bass Clef Edition $22.99
00842042 Treble Clef Edition $16.95

HOW TO PLAY FROM A REAL BOOK
by Robert Rawlins

Explore, understand, and perform the songs in real books with the techniques in this book. Learn how to analyze the form and harmonic structure, insert an introduction, interpret the melody, improvise on the chords, construct bass lines, voice the chords, add substitutions, and more. It addresses many aspects of solo and small band performance that can improve your own playing and your understanding of what others are doing around you.

00312097 ....$19.99

JAZZ DUETS
ETUDES FOR PHRASING AND ARTICULATION
by Richard Lowell
Berklee Press

With these 27 duets in jazz and jazz-influenced styles, you will learn how to improve your ear, sense of timing, phrasing, and your facility in bringing theoretical principles into musical expression. Covers: jazz staccato & legato • scales, modes & harmonies • phrasing within and between measures • swing feel • and more.

00302151 ....$14.99

JAZZ THEORY & WORKBOOK
by Lilian Dericq & Étienne Guéreau

Designed for all instrumentalists, this book teaches how jazz standards are constructed. It is also a great resource for arrangers and composers seeking new writing tools. While some of the musical examples are pianistic, this book is not exclusively for keyboard players.

00159022 ....$19.99

JAZZ THEORY RESOURCES
by Bert Ligon
Houston Publishing, Inc.

This is a jazz theory text in two volumes. **Volume 1 includes**: review of basic theory • rhythm in jazz performance • triadic generalization • diatonic harmonic progressions and analysis • substitutions and turnarounds • and more. **Volume 2 includes**: modes and modal frameworks • quartal harmony • extended tertian structures and triadic superimposition • pentatonic applications • coloring "outside" the lines and beyond • and more.

00030458 Volume 1 ....$39.99
00030459 Volume 2 ....$32.99

JAZZOLOGY
THE ENCYCLOPEDIA OF JAZZ THEORY FOR ALL MUSICIANS
by Robert Rawlins and Nor Eddine Bahha

This comprehensive resource covers a variety of jazz topics, for beginners and pros of any instrument. The book serves as an encyclopedia for reference, a thorough methodology for the student, and a workbook for the classroom.

00311167 ....$24.99

MODALOGY
SCALES, MODES & CHORDS: THE PRIMORDIAL BUILDING BLOCKS OF MUSIC
by Jeff Brent with Schell Barkley

Primarily a music theory reference, this book presents a unique perspective on the origins, interlocking aspects, and usage of the most common scales and modes in occidental music. Anyone wishing to seriously explore the realms of scales, modes, and their real-world functions will find the most important issues dealt with in meticulous detail within these pages.

00312274 ....$24.99

THE SOURCE
THE DICTIONARY OF CONTEMPORARY AND TRADITIONAL SCALES
by Steve Barta

This book serves as an informative guide for people who are looking for good, solid information regarding scales, chords, and how they work together. It provides right and left hand fingerings for scales, chords, and complete inversions. Includes over 20 different scales, each written in all 12 keys.

00240885 ....$21.99

HAL•LEONARD®
www.halleonard.com

ARTIST TRANSCRIPTIONS

Artist Transcriptions are authentic, note-for-note transcriptions of today's hottest artists in jazz, pop and rock. These outstanding, accurate arrangements are in an easy-to-read format which includes all essential lines. **Artist Transcriptions** can be used to perform, sequence or for reference.

FLUTE

00672379	Eric Dolphy Collection	$19.95
00672582	The Very Best of James Galway	$19.99
00672372	James Moody Collection – Sax and Flute	$19.95

GUITAR & BASS

00660113	Guitar Style of George Benson	$19.99
00672573	Ray Brown – Legendary Jazz Bassist	$22.99
00672331	Ron Carter Collection	$24.99
00660115	Al Di Meola – Friday Night in San Francisco	$24.99
00125617	Best of Herb Ellis	$19.99
00699306	Jim Hall – Exploring Jazz Guitar	$19.99
00672353	The Joe Pass Collection	$22.99
00673216	John Patitucci	$22.99
00672374	Johnny Smith – Guitar Solos	$24.99

PIANO & KEYBOARD

00672487	Monty Alexander Plays Standards	$19.95
00672520	Count Basie Collection	$19.95
00192307	Bebop Piano Legends	$19.99
00113680	Blues Piano Legends	$22.99
00672526	The Bill Charlap Collection	$19.99
00278003	A Charlie Brown Christmas	$19.99
00672300	Chick Corea – Paint the World	$19.99
00146105	Bill Evans – Alone	$21.99
00672548	The Mastery of Bill Evans	$16.99
00672365	Bill Evans – Play Standards	$22.99
00121885	Bill Evans – Time Remembered	$22.99
00672510	Bill Evans Trio Vol. 1: 1959-1961	$29.99
00672511	Bill Evans Trio Vol. 2: 1962-1965	$27.99
00672512	Bill Evans Trio Vol. 3: 1968-1974	$29.99
00672513	Bill Evans Trio Vol. 4: 1979-1980	$24.95
00193332	Erroll Garner – Concert by the Sea	$22.99
00672486	Vince Guaraldi Collection	$19.99
00289644	The Definitive Vince Guaraldi	$39.99
00672419	Herbie Hancock Collection	$24.99
00672438	Hampton Hawes Collection	$19.95
00672322	Ahmad Jamal Collection	$27.99
00255671	Jazz Piano Masterpieces	$22.99
00124367	Jazz Piano Masters Play Rodgers & Hammerstein	$19.99
00672564	Best of Jeff Lorber	$19.99
00672476	Brad Mehldau Collection	$24.99

00672388	Best of Thelonious Monk	$24.99
00672389	Thelonious Monk Collection	$24.99
00672390	Thelonious Monk Plays Jazz Standards – Volume 1	$24.99
00672391	Thelonious Monk Plays Jazz Standards – Volume 2	$24.99
00264094	Oscar Peterson – Night Train	$22.99
00672544	Oscar Peterson – Originals	$17.99
00672531	Oscar Peterson – Plays Duke Ellington	$27.99
00672563	Oscar Peterson – A Royal Wedding Suite	$19.99
00672569	Oscar Peterson – Tracks	$19.99
00672533	Oscar Peterson – Trios	$39.99
00672534	Very Best of Oscar Peterson	$29.99
00672371	Bud Powell Classics	$22.99
00672376	Bud Powell Collection	$24.99
00672507	Gonzalo Rubalcaba Collection	$19.95
00672316	Art Tatum Collection	$27.99
00672355	Art Tatum Solo Book	$22.99
00672357	The Billy Taylor Collection	$24.95
00673215	McCoy Tyner	$22.99
00672321	Cedar Walton Collection	$19.95
00672519	Kenny Werner Collection	$19.95

SAXOPHONE

00672566	The Mindi Abair Collection	$14.99
00673244	Julian "Cannonball" Adderley Collection	$22.99
00673237	Michael Brecker	$24.99
00672429	Michael Brecker Collection	$24.99
00672529	John Coltrane – Giant Steps	$22.99
00672494	John Coltrane – A Love Supreme	$17.99
00672493	John Coltrane Plays "Coltrane Changes"	$19.95
00672453	John Coltrane Plays Standards	$25.99
00673233	John Coltrane Solos	$29.99
00672328	Paul Desmond Collection	$22.99
00672530	Kenny Garrett Collection	$24.99
00699375	Stan Getz	$24.99
00672377	Stan Getz – Bossa Novas	$24.99
00673254	Great Tenor Sax Solos	$22.99
00672523	Coleman Hawkins Collection	$24.99
00673239	Best of Kenny G	$22.99
00673229	Kenny G – Breathless	$19.99
00672462	Kenny G – Classics in the Key of G	$26.99

00672485	Kenny G – Faith: A Holiday Album	$17.99
00672373	Kenny G – The Moment	$22.99
00672498	Jackie McLean Collection	$19.95
00672372	James Moody Collection – Sax and Flute	$19.95
00672539	Gerry Mulligan Collection	$24.99
00102751	Sonny Rollins, Art Blakey & Kenny Drew with the Modern Jazz Quartet	$17.99
00675000	David Sanborn Collection	$19.99
00672491	The New Best of Wayne Shorter	$24.99
00672550	The Sonny Stitt Collection	$19.95
00672524	Lester Young Collection	$22.99

TROMBONE

00672332	J.J. Johnson Collection	$24.99
00672489	Steve Turré Collection	$19.99

TRUMPET

00672557	Herb Alpert Collection	$19.99
00672480	Louis Armstrong Collection	$22.99
00672481	Louis Armstrong Plays Standards	$22.99
00672435	Chet Baker Collection	$24.99
00672556	Best of Chris Botti	$21.99
00672448	Miles Davis – Originals, Vol. 1	$19.99
00672451	Miles Davis – Originals, Vol. 2	$19.95
00672449	Miles Davis – Standards, Vol. 2	$19.95
00672479	Dizzy Gillespie Collection	$19.95
00673214	Freddie Hubbard	$19.99
00672506	Chuck Mangione Collection	$22.99

HAL•LEONARD®

Visit our web site for songlists or to order online from your favorite music retailer at
www.halleonard.com

Prices, content, and availability subject to change without notice.